Helpful Harry
and other stories

Helpful Harry page 3

The magic hole in the wall page 12

Lucy gets lost page 22

Nelson

Thomas Nelson and Sons Ltd
Nelson House   Mayfield Road
Walton-on-Thames   Surrey
KT12 5PL   UK

51 York Place
Edinburgh
EH1 3JD   UK

Thomas Nelson (Hong Kong) Ltd
Toppan Building 10/F
22A Westlands Road
Quarry Bay   Hong Kong

Thomas Nelson Australia
102 Dodds Street
South Melbourne
Victoria 3205   Australia

Nelson Canada
1120 Birchmount Road
Scarborough Ontario
M1K 5G4   Canada

© Macmillan Education Ltd 1987
This edition © Thomas Nelson & Sons Ltd 1992
Editorial Consultant: Donna Bailey
'Helpful Harry' was written by Griselda Gifford and illustrated by Linda Birch
'The magic hole in the wall' was written by Griselda Gifford and illustrated by Shirley Bellwood
'Lucy gets lost' was written by Graham Jameson and illustrated by Lynne Willey

First published by Macmillan Education Ltd 1987
ISBN 0-333-41890-5

This edition published by Thomas Nelson and Sons Ltd 1992

ISBN 0-17-400617-9
NPN 9 8 7 6 5 4

All rights reserved. No paragraph of this publication may be reproduced, copied or transmitted save with written permission or in accordance with the provisions of the Copyright, Design and Patents Act 1988, or under the terms of any licence permitting limited copying issued by the Copyright Licensing Agency, 90 Tottenham Court Road, London W1P 9HE.

Any person who does any unauthorised act in relation to this publication may be liable to criminal prosecution and civil claims for damages.

Printed in Hong Kong

Helpful Harry

"Harry is too bouncy," Mum said.
"Harry is just naughty," Dad said.
Harry heard them and was sad.
He only wanted to be helpful.

He took all the dirty wheels off his toy cars and washed them in the bath.
It was not his fault that the small wheels went down the plug-hole, was it?

The dog would not eat his food, so Harry ate some to show the dog that it was good. Why did that make Mum so cross?

The goldfish looked very hungry, so Harry
fed them a whole packet of chocolate biscuits.
How was he to know that Gran was coming to tea?
And then the goldfish got ill and lay on the bottom
of the bowl, so Mum had to change the water.
But Harry had only tried to be helpful.

Mum had a bad headache, so Harry
cut off all the tops of the tulips to make
a nice bunch of flowers for her.
But Mum was cross and told him not to do it again!

Then he mixed Mum's powder and scent and
some soapflakes and some cornflakes
to make a nice pudding for her.
But he couldn't help it if he had used up all her
best scent and spilled her powder on the carpet.
"What a mess Harry," said Mum.
She was very, very cross with him.

"Do try to be good Harry," Mum said one day. He had a new baby sister who cried a lot and Mum was very busy.

Just then the baby cried again and Mum rushed to the cot.

"Do you want a little boy now?" Harry said sadly as he watched her hold the baby.
Mum smiled at him.

"Of course I do Harry darling. Just be good and helpful while I am so busy," she said.

Harry wanted to be good.
He wanted to be helpful.
He went into the kitchen and
put all the dirty dishes in the bowl.
He would wash them up.
He poured in lots of lovely washing-up soap.
He turned on the tap.
Soon there was a great deal of soapy water.
Harry stood on a chair and began to wash up.
He got very wet, but he did want to be helpful.

Then he looked out of the window
and saw a ladder.
Dad had been painting the house.
Harry wanted to help.
He found a tin of paint and the brush.
Washing-up was boring.
Painting would be fun and helpful.
It was very hard to open the tin.
He used Mum's best spoon.
The spoon did get a bit bent, but
he got the tin open.
At last he dipped his brush into
the lovely squidgy blue paint.

Then he climbed the ladder.
He climbed very slowly because
it was a long way from one step to another.
Here was the bedroom window.
There was Mum feeding the baby.
Harry held on tight with one hand.
With the other hand he lifted up the brush.
He put a big blob of blue paint on the window.
The handle was rather slippery and
then he dropped the brush.
   Someone called him. He looked down.
It was Gran and – oh dear!
Her white hair was now blue and white!
The brush had fallen on her head!

"Come down at once Harry," Gran cried.
Harry thought the ground was a long way off.
He was scared and he screamed.
So did Mum when she looked up and saw him.
Mum helped Harry down the ladder.
She got the paint out of Gran's hair.
She mopped the floor where the water had spilled because of Harry's washing-up.
"You are bad Harry," Mum said.
Harry was sad. He only wanted to help.

In the afternoon he went with Mum to the park.
Mum was tired and sat on a seat in the sun.
The baby was asleep in her pram.
Harry ran down the hill.
When he came back, a dog was sniffing
at the pram wheels.
The pram moved, going down the hill!
Harry ran after it. He jumped and
caught the pram handles.
At last it stopped. Mum ran up.
"Harry!" she cried. She hugged him.
"You saved the baby," she said.
Harry was very happy.
At last he had been helpful.

The magic hole in the wall

    Mandy was bored. She missed her old home and her friend Sarah.
    "There is nothing to do here," she said.
    She looked at the dull little garden.
Her old garden had been big.
It had a sandpit and thick bushes
to play hide and seek.
There was only a tall old wall round this garden
and big houses all round.

"What shall I do?" Mandy asked her mother.
Mum was busy unpacking.
"I can't play with you now," she said.
"Why not dig a little garden for yourself?"
Mandy thought she would dig for treasure.
She took her beach spade and dug
in the hard, sooty earth.
All she found was a dog's bone and a tin lid.

"I will climb the wall," she said to herself.
She tried, but she was too small.
All she did was to pull a loose brick out.
  She looked through the hole in the wall.
It would be fun to see into the next garden.
She saw some light. Someone had taken away
the brick on the other side.
But something blocked the light in the middle.

Mandy put her hand in the hole.
She took out a doll made of red plasticine.
Whose was it?
Then she found a toy dumper truck.
Someone had left them for her.
It was like magic!

She played with the dumper truck,
making roads in the garden.
She squashed up the big doll into a ball.
Then she made two little dolls out of it.

"Magic dolls," she said.

   Mandy went back to the wall to see if
the magic had left any more toys.
She looked through the hole.
Two large brown eyes stared back at her
from the other side!
Tears fell out of the eyes.
   "You have stolen my toys," said a little girl.
Mandy took the dumper truck and the red dolls.
She put them back in the hole in the wall.

"Here they are," she said. "I'm sorry.
I thought magic left them for me.
I have made two red dolls instead of the big one.
I am Mandy."

"I am Sue," said the little girl.
A hand took the dolls and the truck.

"I liked the big doll, but the little ones
are nice too," said Sue.

"Can you come and play?" Mandy said.
I have made roads for your truck."
"I will ask my Mum," said Sue.
"And I will tell mine," said Mandy.

"I have found a new friend," she said to her Mum.
Just then the door bell rang.
It was Sue and her mother.
"You must be busy unpacking," said Sue's mother.
"You won't want Sue playing here."
She looked at all the boxes in the hall.

"Of course Sue must come and play,"
said Mandy's mother. "Mandy is lonely here."
Mandy took Sue into the garden.
It was not boring now that Sue was here.
They played with the dumper truck.
They dug a garden.
"We will grow magic sunflowers," Sue said.
They planted the seeds.
"The flowers will grow higher than the wall,"
said Sue. "Like magic."

The next day Mandy looked at the hole in the wall. She found a piece of paper. It said COME TO TEA.

Sue's garden was full of flowers.
There was a swing and a sandpit.
Sue had a dog called Sally.
They chased Sally round the garden.
They swung high on the swing.

"I can see over the wall," said Mandy.

Each day Sue played with Mandy.
Sometimes they talked through the hole in the wall.
The sunflowers grew higher than the wall.

On Mandy's birthday, she went to the wall.
She found a little parcel there.
The label said LOVE FROM SUE.
There were magic paper flowers inside
that opened in water.
There was a magic painting book and magic sweets
that changed colour when you sucked them.

"I am glad we came here," said Mandy, "and I found
my magic hole in the wall!"

Lucy gets lost

On Saturday morning, Lucy and her Dad set off for the market.
Dad was going to cook snapper fish with peppers and rice for supper.

When they got to the market, they couldn't find anywhere to park the car.

"Let's just leave it here outside the church," said Dad.

"But we're opposite the police station," said Lucy. "Won't you get a parking ticket?"

"Oh, they're too busy to bother with us," said Dad. "We'll take a chance. We won't be long."

"All right," said Lucy. "But remember you got a ticket last time."

The market was very busy and noisy. Lucy felt a little frightened by the noise and the crowds. She held on tightly to Dad's hand.

Suddenly she heard a voice say, "Hey Clive, Lucy. What's happening?"

She looked up and saw Dad's friend Maxie. Dad and Maxie shook hands and Maxie patted her on the head. Soon Dad and Maxie were having one of their long talks together. Lucy decided to leave them to it and have a look around.

Just across from where she was standing was a fruit and vegetable stall.
There was every different kind and colour of fruit and vegetables you could think of and some Lucy had never seen before.

Next to it she found an even more interesting stall, the pet stall.
It had guinea-pigs and hamsters and cages full of brightly coloured budgies.
But best of all were some lovely soft puppies.

Lucy played with the puppies for a while and then turned round to look for Dad.
But Dad and Maxie weren't there where she had left them. She couldn't see them anywhere.
She was lost!

For a moment she felt stuck to the spot with fear. Her tummy seemed to turn over inside. She bit her lip and a big tear fell slowly down her cheek. Lucy felt very lonely and afraid, surrounded by all these people.

Then she said to herself, "This is silly. Dad was so busy talking to Maxie that he's walked off towards the fish stall, still talking, and he thinks I'm still behind him." So she set off for the fish stall.

But when she got to the fish stall,
there was no Dad and no Maxie.
There were lots of different kinds of fish and
even a big red snapper resting on a pile of ice.
But no Dad.
 Lucy felt very worried now.
She stuck her thumb firmly in her mouth
like she always did when she was troubled.
Then she went up to the man in the straw hat and
apron who kept the fish stall.

"Please, have you seen my Dad?" she said.

"Well, my dear," said the man. "I've seen lots of people, but if you're lost, we had better tell the policeman over there."

"Oh dear," thought Lucy. "Maybe I'll get into trouble, or maybe Dad will for losing me," so she began to run.

"Come back!" said the man. "You'll only get more lost."

But Lucy kept on running.
She had decided what to do.
She would go back to the car and
wait for Dad to turn up.

But when she got to the car, Dad was not there. Someone else was though. It was a traffic warden. She was writing out a ticket for Dad's car.
Lucy suddenly thought, "Perhaps Dad will never come back," and she started to cry long and hard.

The traffic warden was very kind.

"What's up?" she said and gave Lucy a cuddle. Lucy told her the whole story.

Just as Lucy had finished, she looked across the busy street and saw two men rushing towards the steps of the police-station.
She gave a little cry as she recognised Dad and Maxie. She began to wave and shout.

"Stay here Lucy," said the lady. "I'll get them for you," and she hurried across the road towards Dad and Maxie.

Lucy saw the lady tap Dad on the shoulder.
He turned around.
She saw the lady talking to Dad and
pointing across the street towards her.
Dad stopped and looked and waved and waved.
It seemed as if his arm would drop off.
Then he came rushing across the road so quickly that
he nearly got knocked over by a bus and
a paper parcel fell out of his pocket.

When he got to the car he picked Lucy up and gave her a big hug.

Just then the lady came up to them and said, "I think you dropped this."

She handed Dad the paper parcel.

Dad said, "Oh yes. Thank you."

He opened the parcel and there inside was a beautiful red snapper fish.

"You've been very kind," said Dad.

"I'm glad I could help," said the lady.
"You've got your little girl back now and
you've got this lovely fish for tea.
I remember when I was a little girl,
my mother used to cook fish on Saturday nights
with rice and peppers."

"Dad," said Lucy thoughtfully. "I think
we should say thank you to the lady."

"Oh yes," said Dad. "So we should.
Lucy and I would like you to accept this as a gift,"
said Dad and he gave her the fish.

"Oh dear, thank you very much," said the lady.
"But in return I'm afraid I have to give you this,"
and she handed Dad a parking ticket.